28 Days To A New Me:
A Journey of Commitment

Robert Kennedy III

DEDICATION

Nadia, you have supported EVERY dream I have ever had.
You're with me when I'm excited and when I'm not so excited.
Thank you for sticking with me as I discover the NEW ME!! Love
you babe!

Coach George, dude you just don't KNOW!! The relationship that
we have developed has been instrumental in this. I thought that I
was a risk taker before we met. But, you've inspired some STUFF
man and helped me chip away at things I did not realize existed.
You're awesome bro!

CONTENTS

PREFACE

"You can't wait for a perfect day to begin. Now is as good a time as any......"

-RK3

Who knew that this would actually turn into a "thing"? This whole idea came out of the study of habits. I was doing some reading and posted on Facebook something about it taking 28 days to form a habit. I followed that up with the question, "What new habits are you going to form?" I was totally unprepared for the firestorm of answers much less the fact that so many wanted change and needed help. Well, I committed to help and so here we are.

This is not all my doing, though. I couldn't have made this happen without some great people. So, I'd like to shout out:

Nadia Kennedy (my wife, my inspiration, my lover, my best friend), Rayleen Weatherly (the other critical mind behind this), George Watson (my coach), Robert & Seslie Kennedy (my parents), Leighton & Sheldon (two of the most supportive brothers a guy could want), critical eyes like Sandra Hinds, Angel Jean-Louis, Jennifer Pelletier (you helped beyond belief), Nicki Steinberger and key entrepreneurial supporters like April Williams (Kennedy Consulting), Shawn Chevalier (Hardbody Outdoor Fitness), Chip Dizard, Lois Peters, Dr. Marcellus Cephas. A special shout out goes to Rich Murphy for helping me with my first book and opening my eyes a bit to this world of writing.

Of course, the kids are going to ask me, "Daddy, is my name in the book?"

Hey kids! Yup, you're here! I didn't forget you! Love you guys!

What Will You Need?

Press forward. Do not stop, do not linger in your journey, but strive for the mark set before you.

~ George Whitefield

This 28 day journey is one of commitment. You will learn quite a bit about yourself. You will re-learn the definition of some words and concepts. If you pay attention, you will even find out a bit more about your own mental makeup. This only works if you remain committed throughout the 28 day process. Each stop or break allows for a pause that works against your commitment. But, don't let that be an excuse or detractor. Pick it right back up and continue moving forward.

".....strive for the mark set before you!"

As you go through each day, you may need:

1. 28 index cards or something creative that can serve the same purpose

2. A pen or writing utensil

3. Tape, push pins or something to be able to post your cards

4. Somewhere to post your proof. You will need to create a visual map of the journey. There are many resources to do this on your own. You can do something as simple as signing up for a Flickr account, posting to a private

Facebook album or uploading your proofs to a Google Drive account. You may even consider printing out your photos or files and storing them in a physical folder if that works for you.

Writing is a critical piece of this journey. Be sure to complete the daily actions.

The First 7 Days

Every journey has a beginning point. Some end and others simply transition. This journey is not about right or wrong. It's simply about making a commitment and then being in action on that commitment. Are you ready? NO EXCUSES!! Let's move!

Day 1 – Let's GO!

28 Day PARAMETERS

1. *Choose a commitment (Some of you might prefer the term goal, but we will deal with that later)*

2. *Commit to an action for 28 straight days*

3. *Make NO EXCUSES*

4. *Perform your action everyday*

5. *Get a journal file (a word document, a Google doc) Post your thoughts about the action daily*

6. *Prove your actions daily through a picture, a document/file, a video (or any means that shows your progress other than simply saying, "I did it")*

Consider this: Everything that you have done up to this point has gotten you to where you are. If that is working for you, AWESOME!! If not, then it's time to try something different. My thought is that you simply decide that you are going to get into action and then you do it! Here's the plan, do it for 28 Days! Every day!

First, let's look at where you are currently. What is it that you want to do? What is missing in your life? Get a piece of paper. Then, set a timer for 5 minutes. Write down everything that you can think of regarding where you are today and what your life is like. Don't distinguish anything. Don't think about good, bad, or ugly. Just write.

Once you have completed that, write down your goal and what you are going to commit to for the next 28 days. Finished? Awesome!

Now, let's write down your baseline. With regard to your commitment, what are you doing now? Write a clear and positive statement indicating where you are. If you are looking to lose weight, write down your current weight and the date. If you are committing to read a book, write down the date and how many pages or chapters you have read. If you are planning to take on doing something for your spouse daily for the next 28 days, write down what it is and how often you currently perform that action.

The big thing here is putting a number to everything that you do. You will need to see clearly how much time, how often and even what time. This is going to be one of the most important journeys that you can ever take for yourself, a journey into commitment.

LOCK IN! SADDLE UP! This is YOUR journey! Picture yourself as a winner. Lock into the picture of you in 28 days.

I won't be able to check in with you every day, mainly because I can't see you. But, here's how you can use this book. Set a time every day that you are going to read the section for that day. After you have read and completed the activity listed, get moving on your goal.

Day 2 - No Excuses

Pick Me-Up Line

I attribute my success to this: I never gave or took an excuse.

- Florence Nightingale

What do you mean NO excuses? Dude, I can't help it if I got sick. I can't help it if I got rear ended by a crazy driver. I can't help it if the kids have birthday parties and 400 appointments in the same day. That JUST doesn't leave me any room to do my own stuff. You know what? You are abso-tively-right! That definitely doesn't leave any room. But since when did life just conveniently leave you room to "do your own stuff?"

You "do your stuff" in spite of life. Yes, I know that it may sound harsh, but the honest truth is that life just happens with or without you. That time that you were waiting for, when you had a little bit of time to spare, when the cavalry was coming to save you, isn't coming. Are you willing to accept that today? Great. Now, that's out of the way, we can get to some good news. The good news is you can still create, generate and take action in SPITE of that stuff. You can only control you. You can only take 100% responsibility for you and everything that you are involved with. You are the only person that can cause your action or pause your action.

I read a statement by Steve Chandler in his book, 100 Ways To Motivate Yourself. It said something to the effect of life is either about creation or reaction. You get to decide which one. Notice that "conveniently" the letters for each are the same. You get to control the 'c'. It's one or the other. If you are not creating, you are reacting. There is no in between. It starts mentally. And likewise, you are either committed or you are not. There is no in between. And there are no excuses either. Ahhhh! Embrace it! It's actually pretty refreshing. Welcome to Commitment!

TODAY'S ACTION

1. Take a card/piece of paper and write down your ONE commitment

2. On the back of that Card/Paper, make a list of 5 - 10 reasons why you have not been able to do this before (at least the reasons that you have told yourself - i.e., was tired, not enough time, etc.)

3. Place a BIG X through those reasons and then write NO MORE EXCUSES at the top of the card/paper.

Day 3 – Find Your Way To Service

Pick Me-Up Line

Wherever a man turns he can find someone who needs him.

- Albert Schweitzer

OK. So, I've screwed up so many times that I can't even begin to count them anymore. You know that comment about God numbering the hairs on your head and knowing the number of stars in the sky? Yes, that's about the number of times I have screwed up. I've especially screwed up when I've tried to become disciplined about something in my life. I've messed up every time I've tried to get on an exercise program. I've screwed up my budgeting. I've owed people money. I've said things that haven't turned out how I planned. I've meant well, but I've screwed up.

But, I think I have figured out part of why things have been so hard in many cases. You ready for this? I really think that it was because I made it about me. Huh? Yes, exactly! I made it about me. You see, I was trying to do something to make myself better. Or, I was trying to do something to take care of me. Or, I was trying to do something just so that I wouldn't be embarrassed or look bad. I was trying to do something on my own because I felt I had to. However, the moment that I turned something outward to someone else, I found it easier to maintain my commitment. I am sitting here writing this and I find it easier to write this morning because I am not writing for money or for me. I am writing for you. My goal in writing this is simply to give hope to someone else or to help someone see a new perspective.

Every time that I have determined to do something for someone else, it has been successful. Every time that I have started an exercise program and aimed to help someone else be consistent in their exercise or health as well, I have been successful. I'm not sure of the science behind this but it seems that there is a passion chemical that goes into effect whenever you decide to help someone else or be of service. The moment you take the focus off yourself, the passion chemical kicks in. It becomes so much easier to do what you are doing because it's not about you anymore. It's about someone else.

So, if you want to find a way to stick to it, a way to be committed, find your way to service. Serve someone else! Try it. Walk out your door this morning and buy a bagel for the guy that's sitting outside Starbucks. Call someone up just to say hey. Send your spouse an unexpected text message. Do something today that serves someone else. You'll be amazed. Try it!

TODAY'S ACTION

1. Find someone else (a friend, a family member) that is committed to exercise or another program.

2. Send them an encouraging text, email or phone call.

Day 4 – Resisting Resistance

Pick Me-Up Line

Paralyze resistance with persistence.

- Woody Hayes

Have you ever been driving your car and you drive by someone that's running? I know that I have and there are times where I think, "Man, that person must just LOVE running!"

Conversely, there are times when I drive by someone who looks like they are struggling and I think that they must absolutely HATE themselves when they get back home. But, they are doing it. They are in ACTION. I don't know if you have ever talked to someone who is training for a marathon or someone who runs a lot. But, when I've asked the question, "How do you motivate yourself to get up every morning to do this?", the response I usually get is, "By getting up every morning to do this." Huh? You would think that some people just have a different drive and are just more motivated than others, right? Nope!! Some people are just more in action than others. That's the trick. That's the thing!! People who run FEEL like running once they are actually running. But, most still have to drag themselves out of bed, maybe saying affirmations or just talking to themselves saying, "REALLY, you GOTTA GET UP!!"

It's not easy, but it's simple! You don't necessarily feel like being in action. You just do it!! That sound familiar? Yes, that

Nike slogan has permeated our lives for at least the past 2 decades (Well, if you're that old anyway). What it's really saying is that you won't always FEEL like getting in action. DO IT ANYWAY. You won't always FEEL like running. DO IT ANYWAY! You won't always FEEL like changing your diet. DO IT ANYWAY!

I read a book by Steven Pressfield called the War of Art. He talks about the concept of Resistance. Anything that is important to you, anything that you have committed to will bring resistance. This doesn't necessarily come from others. This doesn't mean that people will tell you not to do what you are committed to doing. This resistance is just a seemingly natural force that occurs and it appears in the form of fear many times. When it appears, we often make excuses like "I'm tired" or "I deserve a break, I've been working hard" or "It's too late" or "but I have to do this with the kids" or .... do you get it? Resistance will come in all forms of "legitimate" excuses. The key here is resisting resistance. You've got to push through. Recognize it for what it is and then DO IT ANYWAY!! You've made a commitment. Get in action! Something's ALWAYS going to pop up! Don't let it stop you! GO!

TODAY'S ACTION

1. Take a moment to think about your commitment.

2. Think about 3 things that could get in the way of you completing your commitment and then write those down.

3. Now, write down 3 ways that you can complete your commitment creatively in spite of those obstacles.

Day 5 - Performing: Keeping It Black & White

Pick Me-Up Line

An ounce of performance is worth pounds of promises.

- Mae West

"I didn't get to exercise today because I was busy."

"I couldn't follow my proper diet today because I didn't have enough vegetables."

"I was late because there was an accident on the highway today."

"I didn't finish the project because the dog ate my pencil."

Now, most of these are legitimate things. There are things in life that you just can't avoid some times. There are other things that you CAN avoid if you prepare better for them. But we can't prepare for EVERYTHING, can we? Guess what, it doesn't matter. WHAT?? What on earth do you mean it doesn't matter?

Here's a story. Let's say that you are running a race, let's call it the New York City Marathon. You have been running for 2 solid hours, you are in first place and you are well ahead of the 2nd place person. About 50 yards from the finish line, a dog runs out on to the course and runs into your path. In trying to avoid the dog, you stumble and fall, hurting your knee pretty badly in the process. You try to crawl forward to the finish line but you are just in too much pain. So, you ask for assistance. As the medical staff comes to help you up, the second place runner passes you and you helplessly watch as they break the tape at the finish line. Did you win the race? Nope!! Certainly not. Would you have won if the dog hadn't crossed your path? Probably. Could the race organizers take this into consideration and award you the prize anyway? Possibly. But the fact is that the image of the other runner breaking that tape can never be erased. They won. You lost. It doesn't matter why!! It's what happened. Fair? Probably not!! But fair is not what we are talking about. We are talking about what IS.

Too often, we commit to something and then we live in a world of why it happened and/or why it didn't. Valid or not, progress is based on WHETHER movement happened or not rather than WHY it did or did not happen.

So, if commitment and progress are the streets that you are headed towards, your world has to be one of performance, a black and white world, no grey, no in-between. Keep it simple! Perform! Get in action! Skip the reasons! Just go for it!

TODAY'S ACTION
   1. Get out your calendar.

   2. Look at your next 7 days and place a specific time slot on your calendar every day for the

next 7 days to complete you commitment. You may calendar further if you wish.

Day 6 - Staying Motivated

Pick Me-Up Line

Life takes on meaning when you become motivated, set goals and charge after them in an unstoppable manner.

- Les Brown

If you were to conduct a survey with many people who have failed at an exercise or diet program, the number one reason they would give for that failure is that they were just not "motivated" to continue. They need to work out with someone else to stay motivated. They need to stop watching all the yummy commercials on TV. They wake up tired. They just feel worn down and they are not "motivated" to get up off the couch.

Let's look back at the example of the runner for a moment. I asked them how they got motivated every day to get up out of their bed and run. Their answer? By getting up out of the bed and running. Action. There is no magic pill that makes you FEEL like running. As a matter of fact, many times you don't feel like running until you are actually running. So the "trick" that they have learned is to simply DO IT!! There is a reason that the Nike slogan has been around for so long. It stuck, not just because it's catchy, but because it's also true! Just get into action! Feelings are not a part of the equation. Just get it going, bro (or sis, whichever you prefer).

As the son of a preacher, I often heard my dad break down a biblical word from the Greek, the Hebrew or the Latin. So, I suppose it may just be a part of my makeup to want to try this. In looking up the Latin for the word motivation, I found that the root was motus. This simply means to put into action or to move. This is the same root for the English word motion. So, essentially movement. What that means is that motivation takes place hand in hand with movement. It's not something that you wait around for BEFORE movement takes place. It happens AFTER you decide to take an action. The runner is not motivated to run. They simply decide to run, get in action on it and then they are motivated to continue running and also continue the same action the next day.

So, if you are waiting around for the feeling to hit, STOP!! The feeling is not going to come! If you are sitting on the couch or lying in bed, GET UP!! GO! DO IT! Whatever that thing is that you are committed to, just get up NOW and go do it. If you committed to doing it for 15 minutes, focus on doing it for 1 and then 1 more and then 1 more until you reach that commitment. Part of the fear factor might be that we attempt to take in HUGE chunks of goals. Clear your mind, step back, then step forward focusing only on what you are committed to at that moment. Performing may not get easier, but it becomes easier to make the decision to go once you have formed the habit.

TODAY'S ACTION

1. Think about someone successful that you admire. If you don't have one, find someone.

2. Look up their story on google or wikipedia.

3. Write down the "thing" that they said motivated them to succeed.

4. Write down one thing that you can use in your life to encourage you to success.

Day 7 - The Plans Of A Focused Man

Pick Me-Up Line

To conquer frustration, one must remain intensely focused on the outcome, not the obstacles.

- T.F. Hodge, From Within I Rise: Spiritual Triumph Over Death and Conscious Encounters with "The Divine Presence"

The plans of a diligent man will bring profit. I can change that a bit to say that the plans of a FOCUSED man brings profit. That profit can be financial or it may simply bring something else that is meaningful. But, there can be no denying that focus is critical to growth, progress, accumulation or profit. This opening line comes from Proverbs 21:5.

If you have used Google or lived for over 15 years, you have probably seen a ton of stories regarding focus. There is the story about using a magnifying glass and focusing the sun on a blade of grass. Once the sun is focused intently on the grass, it lights a fire. There is the story of pouring water out of a hose. Once you attach a nozzle to focus the water, the force becomes greater. There is great power or great force that comes when you are focused. Every successful person has this in common....FOCUS.

So why is it so hard to FOCUS? Well, it's like anything else. It takes a bit of practice. We do it all the time without thinking. Wanna watch some TV? Focused. Wanna watch a football game? FOCUSED! Have a craving? Wanna go get some food? FOCUSED!! So, what about the things that you actually WANT to do in order to improve yourself? Well, there's that resistance thing again. Resistance just seems to know when you need to do something important, when you are committed to something. But, it doesn't have to beat you. Once you realize that it's SUPPOSED to be there, then you can recognize it and then FOCUS! It's possible! It's do-able! What do you want? Who are you trying to serve/help? Who are you planning to be? FOCUS!

TODAY'S ACTION

1. Set a timer for 4 minutes. Start the timer. Close your eyes. Breathe in deeply for a few moments. Begin to visualize a picture of what life would be like once you have completely reached or sold out to your commitment. Focus in on the words you see, the sounds you hear, the emotions you feel.

2. Set the timer for 1 minute. Write as much about your focused vision as you can.

Week 2: CPR Days 8-14

The first week is done but you may be starting to feel the burn a bit. You may be even be looking to quit. Focus in this week and get your 28 Days **CPR**.

Day 8 - You Need CPR

Pick Me-Up Line

You don't need to be PERFECT, just PERSISTENT!

- RK3

I need CPR?? Wait a minute...you must be trying some sort of slick analogy, right? Because, if I needed CPR, I wouldn't actually know it, would I? Well, if you were awake, having someone pumping your chest and possibly cracking a rib or two might not be something you would take kindly to. But, saving your life might be something for which you were grateful. I'm just going on a hunch.   Silliness aside, I can't seem to think of anyone I've ever met who has had a goal or commitment and did not struggle with it at some point. In fact, many people get to the point of giving up on it when things hit the fan or when the challenge/resistance comes.

CPR involves some of the key ingredients to resuscitate those journeys and stories that have reached a failure point.

C = Commitment

P = Persistence

R = Responsibility (100%)

It's easy to talk about commitment and that's just what we have been doing. The problem is that some people assign a right/wrong to commitment and there really isn't. Either you are committed to something or not. If you are, GREAT. If not, then ok. Maybe you just weren't ready. The point is that we determine what we want to accomplish and then WE commit to it. If you mess up, so what. Jump back on the wagon and keep moving. The commitment doesn't stop when you fail. The commitment stops when you stop moving towards that thing you are committed to. So, the first ingredient here is commitment.

Speaking of screwing up, I just alluded to the second thing....PERSISTENCE. It's worth saying again. PERSISTENCE! Do you know who are the most persistent people that you'll ever meet? Kids. I know that many parents teach their kids to ride bikes by pushing them and running along with them. That works for some kids. But, I had the pleasure of watching my daughter learn how to ride by her simple persistence. She asked me one day to take off her training wheels. At first, I only took off one of them. She took her bicycle and rode up and down the driveway until she got it. She fell quite a few times, but no tears were shed. She was COMMITTED to learning to ride this bike and not just learning to ride, it had to be TODAY! After an hour of this, she simply asked me to take off the second training wheel. What do you think happened? More spills and some bruises. Tears? Nope! She wanted to ride! She kept on getting up and doing it until in about 2 hours, she had learned to keep her balance and do a pretty good job of turning without spilling. Persistence goes right along with commitment. You may not be able to be perfect, but you can be persistent.

The R? Responsibility....100 percent. So, what exactly does that mean? We'll revisit this in more detail but simply put, it means that you take control, 100 % responsibility for everything in your life and how you choose to respond to it. It's not your fault per se, but its your responsibility. Things affect us, ultimately, in the way that we choose to let them affect us. Where possible, I choose to affect things instead of them affecting me. I choose to CREATE instead of only REACT. I choose what to say, how to proceed, where to step. The phrase "I couldn't help it" or "it wasn't my fault" doesn't exist in this frame. You commit, you persist and simply take responsibility for everything surrounding your commitment. Scary? Maybe! But then, anything you commit to brings out resistance and fears sometimes. Do fears go away? Some do. Some don't. I still have fears. I'm just not afraid of fear anymore. Make sense?

TODAY'S ACTION

1. Think about a time that you had a goal and failed to reach it. Write one sentence about the goal. Then write down one thing that blocked you from reaching that goal.

2. Take that paper, crumple it up and throw it in the trash while saying out loud, "You won't block me from my goal again, and even if you try, it's just temporary!"

Day 9 - You Are 100% Responsible

Pick Me-Up Line

If you take responsibility for yourself you will develop a hunger to accomplish your dreams.

- Les Brown

I'm the oldest of three brothers and I used to HAAAATE it when I would get in trouble simply for being the oldest. *What?? Dude, how do you get in trouble for being the oldest?* Well, when my brothers would get into mischief and do little things that would cause trouble, if I was around and didn't stop them, I would get in trouble as well, whether I participated or not. Yeah, I didn't think it was fair either. I mean, we all make our own decisions, right? So, WHY would I get in trouble if I was minding my own business? Well, my parents had this weird idea in their heads about me being responsible for what was going on around me as much as possible **sarcasm**. Funny, the federal government has this idea too that I can be charged as an accessory even if I didn't actually commit the crime. Hmmm.

What does all of that have to do with commitment and the journey that you are on? Well, here are a few points:

You can't always control what your environment does but you can definitely control what environment you are in;

You can't control what people do but you can control how you respond to what is done;

If your environment is continually set up to be a certain way, you may not be able to control it but can certainly prepare for it and how you will respond to it.

So, 100% responsibility does not mean that you are at fault. It just means that you take responsibility for how you complete your commitment. If you have a commitment to exercise and you have unexpected visitors, its up to you re-organize your commitment. You can either exercise later or say to your guests, "hey, I'm committed to this and I need to get 10 minutes in."

No one can stop you. You may reach some physical blockers or limitations but your mind is yours and you can always CREATE with your mind. Now, take responsibility, get past the blame and the fault and GO CREATE!!

TODAY'S ACTION

1. Write down one thing that you want to do but feel you have been unable to do.

2. Write down the "reason" you think that you have been unable to do it.

3. Place an X through that reason and CREATE 3 things that would enable you to get past that block/obstacle. Think without limits. Nothing you write is crazy.

Day 10 - You Are Persistent

Pick Me-Up Line

Ambition is the path to success, persistence is the vehicle you arrive in.

- William Eardley IV

I grew up hearing the story of "the little engine that could". The phrase "I think I can" was repeated throughout the story. The point for kids was that even though you may slide back down the hill a bit and it may be slow going, you have to keep on pushing forward to get to the top. If you get into the reasons why a vehicle might not be able to climb a hill, you come up with reasons such as an engine not being powerful enough or the wrong type of tires. Whatever it was that the train lacked, it seemed to make up for in one very STRONG area. This train was not perfect.

Once considered the world's fastest woman, Olympic athlete, Wilma Rudolph was diagnosed with paralysis as a child. This was caused by the polio virus. Since I used the words fastest and Olympic in the first sentence, you already know how the story ends. What we want to focus on, though, is the middle. The middle section includes a person who was born prematurely, who wore a brace because her foot was twisted as a result of the disease, who had additional bouts of polio and scarlet fever all before the age of twelve. This person was someone who was not perfect. Yet, the Olympics!

The United States has 3 major automobile corporations, General Motors, Ford and Chrysler. What many people don't know is that 2 of the 3 came from the same place. Most people know that Henry Ford was the inventor who came up with the car concept which was later developed into the Ford Motor company. However, there was another development that took place later which would cause a new company to come out of Ford. That was the Cadillac company, which was, of course, a beginning component of General Motors. Henry Ford was noted to have spent only some years in elementary school. But, he spent much of his early years on his family farm taking care of his mother. As a young boy, he was known for pulling apart watches and putting them back together again. Henry only had a few years of elementary school education. Henry Ford was not perfect.

We can look at all sorts of stories of success. There are two common things (without fail) in all of those stories. First, there was some significant imperfection that made it difficult to accomplish what most people can only dream of. Second, there was a high level of persistence that allowed them to push forward even with failure constantly staring them right in the eyes.

I'll just end this section with this: You don't have to be PERFECT, just PERSISTENT.

TODAY'S ACTION

1. Outside of the examples that we have mentioned, look up the name of an inventor or someone that you know to be successful.

2. Read their biography (a short version like you might find on Wikipedia).

3. Write down one obstacle they faced.

4. Write down one thing they did to get past that obstacle.

Day 11 - Don't Short Circuit The Process

Pick Me-Up Line

The good life is a process, not a state of being. It is a direction not a destination.

~Carl Rogers

I love my kids. I was a science teacher for about 9 years. Two totally unrelated statements. Well, not exactly. The fact that I am a parent opens me up to the fact that children have an activity at their school called a science fair. Now, science fairs are pretty cool. It is neat to see the kids trying and experimenting with all sorts of things. One year, my daughter decided that she wanted to build a simple electric circuit using some small light bulbs, a battery, some paper clips and some aluminum foil.

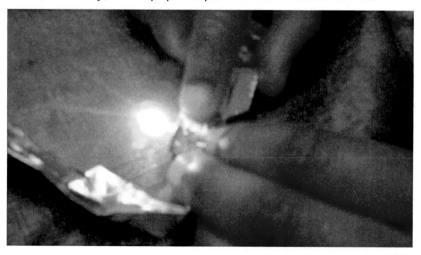

Great project for her. She learned that energy flowing through the foil causes the light to turn on. The foil was connected to both battery ports and then she connected two strands of the foil to the light bulb with paper clips. When she took one end of the paper clip and foil away from the light bulb, the light bulb didn't work anymore. One end was still connected, but there was a break in the process that caused it not to work anymore.

Part of the premise behind this 28 day journey is that it takes 28 days of locked-in commitment to achieve the change you want. Are you going to stop smoking in 28 days? Maybe not. Are you going to be a great husband or wife in 28 days. Possibly and possibly not. Are you going to be a workout fiend in 28 days? Hmmm. I don't know the answer to that. What I DO know is that any broken momentum short circuits the process. Once you get rolling, the process takes over a bit. You will be tempted more. You will have bigger bouts of resistance. You will have more days and times where your mind just tells you "Dude, I don't FEEL like it."

You will also have a head of steam going and a pattern you are forming. Once this pattern begins to lock in, your body and your mind will miss the days that you don't stick to it and they will notify you. In some cases, it comes out as guilt. That's just what your mind is used to.

If you are driving your car at 60 miles per hour, you will travel 60 miles in an hour, provided you don't slow down or stop. Once you stop, pause or get distracted, you've changed the fact. Your car's needle might still say 60 mph but you will no longer get to your destination in 60 minutes. Stopping short-circuited the process a bit.

Another story. When I lived in Massachusetts, I went to a gym with a friend to check it out before we signed up. The owner of the gym gave us a tour around the gym. It was bee-yoo-tee-ful. There were indoor tennis courts, racquetball courts, weight lifting areas, and a good sized pool. There was a list of classes that you could take including spinning, martial arts exercise classes and the list went on. What REALLY grabbed my attention, though, was the fact that when we returned upstairs to where we came in, there was a restaurant. I asked about the menu. Are you ready for this? They sold burgers, fries, nachos, sodas and other fatty delights in this restaurant. The owner's response? "Well, that's just what sells!" In other words, that gym made it really easy to short-circuit the process.

Build your momentum. It's sometimes tough to get the ball rolling but once you do, its easier to maintain. Keep it rolling. Don't break the flow. Don't short-circuit the process. Let that energy make it all the way around the circuit. That's how you continue to achieve the desired results. You're going to be tempted every day. That's part of the process. It's supposed to happen. Recognize it! Then move past it and keep pushing.

TODAY'S ACTION

1. As things get a bit tougher, you may need to build in a new reward system. Get your calendar out and add in a new reward for yourself.

Day 12 - The Two F Words

Pick Me-Up Line

The key to success is to focus our conscious mind on things we desire not things we fear.

- Brian Tracy

One of my favorite stories in the Bible was the story of David and Goliath. Most of us love stories about the underdog and how the underdog wins. But one of the things that I wondered every time I heard the story was how come just one big dude caused an entire army to be afraid. Why was it that one big mouthed guy could stand there yelling and freeze an entire battalion? David came to bring a care package to his brothers who were in the army. He came into a scene where an entire brigade, that I'm sure had four star generals and other highly decorated officers, stood trembling because some huge guy across the valley was yelling at them. Simply put, the big guy provided one element....FEAR.

Now, if you think about it in a non kung-fu movie sense, the army could have gone down and set 10 guys on this one giant and there might have been a different story. But there was something about this guy, in addition to his size, that was causing a fear factor. In my own non-military mind, I always wondered why they didn't just try something different before David came along.

We seem to give that F word, FEAR, a lot of standing in our space. When we give it space, it really does seem to wreck our ability to think clearly and creatively about how to attack a problem. I've heard the saying that reality is usually kinder than our minds make it out to be. We make up all sorts of stories about failure and attach them to ourselves and our situations before anything actually happens. Yep, that F word, FEAR, is smiling!

Let's talk about a different F word. I'll use another Biblical story since we are using them in this section. I'm sure you've heard the story about disciples being out on a boat in a storm. Some of them looked out and saw a man walking on the water towards them. Now, those guys must have been pretty brave because I sure would have started paddling pretty quickly in the other direction. But, enough about my cowardice. As this man came closer, they recognized him to be Jesus. Now, one of the bold guys, Peter, asked to go out and meet Jesus. Of course, Jesus held out His hand and said, "Sure, come on out!"

So, Peter stepped out and what do you know, he started walking on the water too. He took quite a few steps with his eyes locked on Jesus and he was fine. He started to get a bit more comfortable and got a little pep in his step. As a matter of fact, I think he began to do a little dance. As he began one of his twirls, he saw a little lightning and heard a crack of thunder and became afraid. He started to focus on the clouds and then began to sink. What happened? The clouds were there before! What happened? Yep, that first F word, FEAR! He lost his FOCUS, the second F word.

Fear has a way of killing your focus. When you focus on failure or on fear, your focus on the thing you desire becomes impossible to command.

Another story is told about Jimmy Johnson, coach of the Dallas Cowboys and one of his speeches before a Super Bowl. He told his team that if he laid a two by four across the floor of the locker room, most of them would be able to cross it, no problem. But if he laid the same two by four between two buildings, 10 stories high, many would not be able to cross it. Why? The focus was now on falling instead of crossing.

Now, I'm not sure if you can ever dispel fear totally. I like to say that I still have fears, but now I'm just not afraid of fear. Don't let fear kill your focus. FOCUS on your commitment. FOCUS on FINISHING. FOCUS on the moment, don't worry about the future just yet. Envision your success! FOCUS intently! Get glasses. Get a partner. Do whatever you have to do. But FOCUS!

TODAY'S ACTION

1. What is your greatest fear?

2. Write that on a card and place a BIG X through it.

3. Post it where you can see it.

4. What would you like to FOCUS on instead?

5. Write that FOCUS in large letters and place it above that fear.

Day 13 - Making Up Stories

Pick Me-Up Line

Stories can conquer fear, you know. They can make the heart bigger.

- Ben Okri

Have you ever had the chance to run a race? I have and I have had a few experiences where I got to the start line and looked down toward the finish and thought, "MAN, that is SO much further than I thought it would be!" Then, once I had the opportunity to run the race, I looked back and realized that it wasn't so bad. I made up a story.

There was a time in my life when it seemed like $100 was a ridiculous amount of money. So ridiculous, in fact, that I could not envision myself holding a $100 bill without impossible amounts of hard work. But, then one day, I held a $100 bill in my hand and realized that I could find a way to get another one without the impossible journey that I had envisioned before. I made up a story.

When I was a kid, I used to love to watch cartoons (ok, so I still watch them when I get a chance, can't help it). One of the cartoons that I watched was the Jetsons. If you have watched the Jetsons, then you know that it had a world that was made up of flying cars, moving sidewalks, videophones, computers, robots, elevators, an automated life. To my uninitiated kid mind, it was a fantasy, yet, strangely, not an impossibility. I guess, kids have a way of making up stories without making up stories.

I'm rambling or maybe just being flat out confusing now. Here's the explanation. A lot of times, we make up stories about things and change them into something that they are not. We change them into an impossibility or at least a very difficult possibility. All of this before we have attempted anything.

Imagine if we could be in a place where we could simply envision ourselves accomplishing anything. What if I was able to see myself crossing the finish line and then looking back before the race even began? Is that even possible? Well, yes, it is. I would have had to make up a story though.

WHAT? Now, you're confused. Wasn't I just taking about 'making up stories' as the enemy? Not exactly. You see, a race is the distance that it is. It is 100m. It is not long or short, possible or impossible, hard or easy. It is simply 100m. All those other adjectives come via stories that we make up. Now, its simply a matter of which story I want to operate by. Given the choice, I choose the story that makes me a winner EVERY TIME!

This journey is called 28 Days To A New Me. But, if you think about it, you really can make up the story before Day 29. You can create Day 29 right now. You can step INTO Day 29 right now. You can act right now like Day 29 already exists. What are you heading towards? A leaner body? A six pack? A completed book? A healthier marriage? Well, choose THAT story and live in it! Make up the story where you WIN!!

TODAY'S ACTION

1. Write down one thing that you thought was impossible that you have accomplished.

2. Below it, write down what you thought about it once you completed it.

3. Post it on a wall, bulletin board, bathroom mirror or a place where you can see it.

Day 14 - Stretch Yourself

Pick Me-Up Line

"With each passage of human growth we must shed a protective structure [like a hardy crustacean]. We are left exposed and vulnerable - but also yeasty and embryonic again, capable of stretching in ways we hadn't known before."

- Gail Sheehy

When I was a child, I heard what I thought to be some strange statements from my parents sometimes. A few of them related to cars. One that I would hear from my dad, especially when we had to go on a long trip, was that the car had been driven only around the city for a while and it "needed" a long distance trip to keep it in shape. Another one that I heard was that every so often, the car needed to be taken up over the speed limit of 55mph to keep the engine fresh. Now, this was probably my dad's reason to speed a bit sometimes but it still made it fun for me and my brothers.

So, were these fables that parents told me or was there something to it? Well, turns out that in the 80s cars still had engines with carburetors rather than the modern fuel injection engines. The stop and go traffic patterns of the city caused build-up in the carb and a long distance journey allowed some of that to burn off. Today's gas regulations also require that fuel companies place detergents and additives in the gasoline mixture to help with keeping the engine components free from build-up.

What about the speeding? I'm still researching that one. Sorry, I hope you weren't expecting something profound there. Dad's idea though was that anything that performed the same activity in the same way for too long needed to be "stretched" every so often in order for it to be in optimal working condition. Well, maybe optimal is too grand of a word but you get the idea.

You've been pushing on your commitment for 13 days now. It's time to take it out on the track and see what it can do. It's time to stretch just a bit to change the routine just a tad. Stretching yourself is a great way to figure out where you are in the journey. If you have been exercising for 30 minutes per day, pushing to 45 today helps you to see just how far you have come. If you have been running on the treadmill for 30 minutes, taking up the speed a couple of mph for the last 5 mins really puts a bit of test on the muscles. That test, that increase, that gut check helps you and your body and mind recognize that you are capable of a bit more than you were giving yourself credit for up to now. Know what that's called? Growth! That's right, you grow by stretching!

TODAY'S ACTION

1. Look back at what you have been doing for the last 14 days.

2. What can you do to expand your limits?

3. Do something extra today even if you don't "feel" like it.

Week 3: GRIT Days 15-21

WOW!! You've powered through 2 weeks of Commitment!
No excuses, then you got some CPR. You're ready to up your
game. Get some **GRIT!**

Day 15 - Get Your GRIT

Pick Me-Up Line

"....you gotta grit through it because the alternative is unacceptable."

- Chris Christie, Gov. Of New Jersey

I was scarred as a child....traumatized even. Yes, my household was one of those that had porridge so often that even now I run far away from anything that even closely resembles porridge. Oatmeal, instant Quaker cereals and yes, even that southern delicacy, grits!! I know, I know, some of you are reading this and staring in UTTER shock and disbelief that this brother doesn't eat grits. Nope, not even CLOSE. You can put honey on it, dress it up in pretty colors, line the edges with GOLD. Not happening. Doesn't work for me!

While my childhood trauma makes for an interesting byline, we want to get rid of that 'S' and focus in this week on GRIT. The word 'grit' indicates several things like sand, gravel or abrasive particles. But my favorite definition in Webster's dictionary says:

- *firmness of mind or spirit : unyielding courage in the face of hardship or danger*

Two weeks into your commitment, it may be taking something special to reach inside to continue, especially if you are doing an exercise based commitment. Resistance is continuing to kick in and you are wondering when it will get easier. The bad news is that it may not get easier. The good news is that you have become better equipped to handle it and are able to focus just a bit harder to reach this. To make it through, you can reach back and grab a little extra GRIT! You can DO it!!

TODAY'S ACTION

1. Write down your thoughts about the previous two weeks. What have you accomplished? Where have you fallen, if at all?

2. What do you need to do to push through the next two weeks? Write that down.

Day 16 - GRIT: Activate Your Guts

Pick Me-Up Line

Gold medals aren't really made of gold. They're made of sweat, determination, and a hard-to-find alloy called guts.

- Dan Gable

There's this word called *willpower* that a lot of people get caught up in. Some people quit diets, they quit workouts, they quit most things and the excuse that they come up with quite often is that they lack the "willpower." Some people test their willpower by deciding not to have sugar but still keeping a box of donuts on the kitchen counter. The freezer has all sorts of steaks and burgers but, the blame goes to willpower. Here's the thing, willpower is not a feeling that comes over you all of a sudden. Willpower isn't something that was given out at heaven's gate. Willpower is not something that you pick up at the store, pop a battery in and switch on as you are ready to use it.

Now, don't get me wrong, willpower actually exists and can be quite useful. But, I prefer to get at the issue a little earlier in the decision making process. I want to look at the moment where you make a choice, even BEFORE you get into action, the moment where you say YES or NO. I'll use this morning as an example. I set my alarm last night for 5:30AM and this morning, my alarm went off, as all obedient alarms are supposed to, at 5:30AM.

Because the alarm woke me up, (also something it is supposed to do, by the way) I spent a moment in a decision making process that included a few things.

First, I had to decide "Should I allow it to keep ringing?".

Second, I had to decide "Should hit the snooze button?"

Third, I had to answer "Should I do the thing that I asked the alarm to help me do....GET UP?"

My answers were NO, NO, and YES. It took only a split second to make those decisions but they were made. Once I made them, I activated something. I narrowed down my choices. I could now either ignore the choices and make myself a liar. (I'd only be lying to myself, by the way). I could also follow through without delay.

Once I made the decision, I activated my Gut! Yep, my gut! I define GUTS as simply the ability to say Yes or say No in the right situation. Once the Yes or No is out, we have activated something. We have turned on a switch. We have initiated an action of some sort.

Now, I DID say the "RIGHT SITUATION". What situation am I talking about? Well, you commit to something. Whatever needs to happen to line up with that commitment is the "right situation". I committed to waking up so that I could exercise and do some writing. Once I said the appropriate Yesses and Nos, I activated my GUTS. Then, when I was out of bed, most things went a bit more easily from there. Did I want to go back to bed? Heck yeah! Was I thinking about it as I was going to the basement to exercise? Absolutely! Did WILLPOWER kick in to keep me moving towards the basement? Probably! But, it all had to start with a split second YES or NO!

The more you make those decisions, the more used to it your body and mind becomes. That's the whole habit forming thing. It doesn't happen by accident. They are all decisions. Recognize it. Look forward to it. Then simply activate it EVERY TIME! It's inside of us all. You've got GUTS!! Now GO!

TODAY'S ACTION

1. What is the root action that causes you to stumble on your commitments? Is it getting to bed on time? Is it using the snooze button? Is it simple fear of the unknown? Write that down.

2. What one action can you take today that would correct the stumbling?

3. Perform that action right now or create a plan to perform it on your calendar.

Day 17 - Resilience: Get Your Bounce Back

Pick Me-Up Line

In order to succeed, people need a sense of self-efficacy, to struggle together with resilience to meet the inevitable obstacles and inequities of life.

- Albert Bandura

You're afraid of messing up! If that's not true now, it WAS true at some point. We have all experienced the fear of failure. It's natural.

On my wrist, I have a rubber bracelet. It goes everywhere with me. Showers, baths, basketball games, golf, driving, tussling with the kids, you name it.....it stays with me. My kids are young and so they are constantly tugging at it. The cool thing about this bracelet is that every time they tug on it, it simply snaps back into its shape around my wrist. I know, AWESOME, right? Imagine rubber resuming its shape! I know that I have just shared with you some ground breaking science. You're also saying "dude, I've played with MANY rubber bands before and they all break!" But here's why they break. They break because they were doing what they were supposed to do, trying to get back to the shape that they were originally in. When they break, you usually just get another one because you need something that does.......well, what a rubber band does.

Now, back to failure. Some people are petrified of failure, so petrified in fact, that they refuse to move because they are scared of failing. What good is THAT? Here's a secret, something you may not know. Ready? Shhhh, don't tell anyone but.....everyone on the planet has failed at something. Yeah, that's the truth. But, another truth is that failure is necessary for growth. Failure is not an option....its a requirement. That's how we grow. That's how we know what doesn't work. Your tool in this, though, is resilience. Yep, that ol' bounce back. When you hit a rough patch, bounce back. When you get tripped up and make a mistake, yep, BOUNCE back. When you do something and TOTALLY screw it up, that's right, BOUNCE, baby, BOUNCE! Get that rubber band action going and snap back. Bounce back! Get back on track. You're committed. You know where you're going. Get back on the road!

TODAY'S ACTION

1. Get a rubber band and put it on your wrist for the rest of the 28 day journey.

2. Every time you experience a setback or think about not following through on your commitment, lightly pull at it and snap against your wrist as a reminder to bounce back.

Day 18 - Intensity: Grit Your Teeth & Get INTENSE

Pick Me-Up Line

The intensity of your desire governs the power with which the force is directed.

- John McDonald

You know the guy.....the one that you used to laugh at, but you were still jealous of him because of how INTENSE and focused he was. He was so INTENSE that he came off a bit weird. But, you couldn't help admitting that when he was doing whatever it was he was meant to do, he did it well, simply because he was so intensely focused on it. Without fail, intensity is something that ALL of the best athletes and the most successful of us have. They don't only have it at game time, they are also INTENSE during practice. Some people think that is because they just want it really bad. That's definitely true. But, intensity is like going at game speed even in practice. Intensity is putting the time, enthusiasm and energy in even when it may seem like its not important. Intensity is doing what it takes with everything you have.

Have you ever been so focused that someone was calling you and you didn't hear them? So focused that they may have been doing something beside you and you didn't notice? So

INTENSELY focused that they may have even been tapping you on the shoulder and at first you didn't feel it? That's what intensity does. It sheds the obstacles and places you at the finish line before you are physically there. It places you in a world of your creation. It cuts through resistance and places continual action on your commitment.

Don't do it at half speed or with partial focus. Lock in, focus intensely and amp it up today. Get intense!!

TODAY'S ACTION

1. Turn off your phone, your tablet and any other distraction.

2. Close your eyes and clear your mind for 30 secs to a minute.

3. Begin working on your activity/commitment but take it up a notch. FOCUS on it INTENSELY!

Day 19 - Togetherness: Serving Is Winning

Pick Me-Up Line

You will get everything in life that you want if you just help enough other people get what they want.

- Zig Ziglar

No man is an island......It takes a village to raise a child......United we stand, divided we fall.....There are a ton of these, statements that simply talk about the fact that we were not made to do this alone.

I'm going to go back to the creation story where Adam was looking for his companion because all of the other animals and creations had one. There is something inside us, something that triggers an extra level of power when we allow ourselves to be connected to others. Yes, sometimes only ONE person gets the credit, but that's simply because of our human flaws. Yes, sometimes the LEADER gets the accolades but it couldn't happen without the group. The reality is that no matter what we think, there is not a whole lot that we can accomplish, long term, on our own. So, what if I chose to recruit a team from the beginning? What if I chose to curry some favor by simply being helpful?

Individual victories are wonderful. However, the hard fought battles in the trenches with your team are the memorable ones.

There is just a boost that comes out of focusing on someone else and working together. People who volunteer report that they feel strangely rejuvenated when they complete the volunteer task, even though they might be tired. Parents seem to get an odd feeling of "completion" when they do things for their children. My wife will talk about needing a new outfit, yet when she has extra money, she goes out and buys something for our kids or someone else. She gets a kick out of shopping overall but an extra kick, it seems, out of buying things for someone else.

I don't have the definitive answer but it seems that when we serve others, it ends up serving US. In this journey, I recommend focusing on a buddy, a partner, someone else. Take the focus off yourself. It lessens the pressure, allows you to help someone else and in the meantime, you may be accomplish some of your own commitments without recognizing it.

SERVE and you'll WIN.

TODAY'S ACTION

1. Call a friend and simply ask them, "What can I do to help you today?"

Day 20 - Don't Keep It To Yourself

Pick Me-Up Line

If you gossip about yourself, then no one else can talk about you.

- RK3

When I was a kid, every week, after our church service, there was a lady that had a HUGE bag of candy that she would give out to the kids. Now, this COULDN'T have made the parents happy. But, this may have been in the days before they paid attention to hyperactive kids. Our church family called this lady Sister McQueen. But the kids all knew her as.....you guessed it....The Candy Lady!!

The Candy Lady had all sorts of ridiculous goodness in her bag of heavenly treats. However, there were some pieces of candy that were like gold and not as abundant as the others. So, some of the kids would act like they had to go to the bathroom just before the end of the church service so that they could potentially catch The Candy Lady in the hall before she was able to assemble her wares. If you DID happen to catch her, you got to search through the bag without the crowd and you got to take a little more than normal. Once you got your treasure, she would tell you not to tell the other kids yet. Yeah, she knew better than to start a mass exodus and kid riot in the middle of a church service.

Isn't it funny that when you tell people things, they have a way of catching fire? That works REALLY well with the whole gossip thing, doesn't it? So, what is it about doing something positive or helpful that has us wanting to keep it to ourselves?

When you let others know about what you have going on, your commitment, a few things begin to happen. First, they become interested in what you are doing. Second, they most often check in later to see how things are going for you on this commitment. Third, they will potentially tell others about this and others may begin to ask you. Now all of this expecting and telling begins to create a layer of accountability. You are inspiring people with your commitment and they begin to look to you for continued inspiration. Know why? Well, deep down, we all want to accomplish something and we often look to others as a reinforcement that it can actually be accomplished. That's just how it is. That's one reason we have history books. They tell us that other people have done something that was previously thought to be difficult or impossible.

The bottom line here is that people are going to talk about you and your commitment. Why not take it and turn it around? It's going to help them as well as you! Now, don't be shy, put it out there! Shout out that commitment!! GO!

TODAY'S ACTION
1. Tell 3 people about your commitment.

2. Ask them, "If you had to commit to one thing for 28 days, what would it be?"

Day 21 - Focus On The End

Pick Me-Up Line

A goal is a dream with a deadline.

- Napoleon Hill

There are all sorts of mantras or statements that people make about life like 'live like its your last day' or 'just take it one day at a time' or 'put your best foot forward.' These are all action based and I love looking at life through the lens where I get to choose each day and how it happens. The flip side is that it is really easy to say these things, but doing them is sometimes another story. The statements don't always take into account the fact that there are just some things that you don't expect and can't plan for. Things happen. Life happens. When life happens, it can be tempting to get confused, frustrated, discouraged, disparaged and all the other words that essentially mean your plan got screwed up.

That's why it's so important to have a visible focus, a reminder of the direction that are moving in. You have stepped into your new being but you are still moving, looking forward, getting better every day. Your focus is on what you are, on what you are committed to, on the end. That's why self-affirmations begin with 'I am' and not 'I want to be' or 'I'm trying to be'. They focus on the end as if it is now. They bring the future into your present.

Yes, again, that's something easy to say. But the thing about affirmations and life is that the more we repeat actions, the more we see things, the more we hear things, the more it becomes as if that is how it is supposed to be. I don't want to say that it becomes easier. I won't say that the resistance goes away. I will say that you begin to think about the process less and less and after a while you just begin to do.

That's why we talk about the formation of habits. They are powerful. You know this by the fact that it takes so much to break a bad one. So, if you have been on track for the 21 days so far, you should be well on your way to locking in this new you. Keep focused on the end. Keep focused on that future that is now. Live today like you want to be tomorrow. Got it? Good!

TODAY'S ACTION
1. Get an index card

2. Write what Day 29 looks like. Start with 'On Day 29, I am.................."

Week 4: PRESS Method
Days 22 - 28

This is it!! Week 4: THE PRESS METHOD. You need a toolkit to survive each day. Some of those are physical tools. But, the critical one is a mental toolkit that determines how you view and act each day. The **PRESS** method helps you place some valuable items into the kit for easy access.

Day 22 - PRESS Toward Your Mark

Pick Me-Up Line

Press toward the mark for the prize of the high calling.....

- Philippians 3:14

Can you see it? The new you? Yes, that's what I'm talking about. Is that person clearly locked into your gaze? Are you already acting like that person? If not, then jump on into it! First, I want to acknowledge something though. We've spent 3+ weeks talking about commitment and encouraging you to step into the future and bring your future into your present. Here's what I know. It's not easy! Shhhhh, don't tell anybody I admitted that. But, that's the truth. It's not easy. Some people look for a pill or they wonder about guys like me that write this stuff as if it can happen in a moment. It doesn't. I want to be clear that I understand that perfectly. What DOES happen in a moment, though, is your decision. You can take a split second or even less to determine whether you are committed or not. It only takes a fraction to say Yes or No. It takes a really small amount of time to determine whether or not you will get up out of bed, whether or not you will begin to do that jumping jack, whether or not you will pick up that piece of pie to eat it. Those decisions happen really quickly.

Here's the other thing I will acknowledge. You don't only make those decisions once. You can get up out of bed and totally regret the decision 5 seconds later. Then you have to make the decision again. Yeah, AGAIN!! Sometimes you will have to keep making the decision. But, the more you keep making them, the better you become at choosing what works for you and your commitment.

So, show discouragement the DOOR. Give it a good swift kick on the way out. You already know that resistance is coming. You already know that there will be challenges. You already know that it may not get easier to make the decisions. But you also know that you can change your mind at any time in order to make the one that works. Making the decision that works and then putting it to action is the ONLY way to meet your commitment. Yeah, your commitment....remember that thing? You know what's coming. Now PRESS toward your mark for the prize! GO!

TODAY'S ACTION

1. Write down your thoughts about the previous three weeks. What have you accomplished? Where have you fallen, if at all?

2. What do you need to do to push through the next 6 days? Write that down.

Day 23 - PRESS: Positive Language

Pick Me-Up Line

Language is the dress of thought.

- Samuel Johnson

Positive.....first, I want you to get the idea of right or wrong out of your head. When I talk about positive, I am not talking about good versus bad. I am talking about power and control. When someone is investigating something, they might ask you, "Are you sure?" Your response might be, "I'm positive!" Here we are simply talking about being clear, being 100% committed to your answer, being locked into your mental capture of the situation.

Your language, the way you speak, the words that come out of your mouth, have a great deal to do with how you act or respond during the day. Those words tend to come from and help form your mental picture. That picture is what drives how you deal with the world around you. People that believe they have no say in what happens in their world act very differently than those who believe just the opposite. If you have a job, you probably notice that people in leadership positions act very differently than those that are not leading. If there is an "entry level" person that acts like a leader, it probably won't be long before he or she is officially a leader. The way those people "talk" is quite a bit different as well. Many of them talk with a belief, with the idea that there is a way to accomplish something, no matter what the obstacles. To them, the reason that something has flopped is simply because we have found a way that it doesn't work. They believe that we simply need to find a way to make it work. That outlook is evident in the words that come out of their mouth.

How awesome would it be if you never "had" to go to another meeting in your life? That is possible if you change the outlook. Rather than "I have to go to a meeting," saying "I get to go to a brainstorm or an update," indicates that you have a sense of investment, involvement and power over the situation and your feeling surrounding it. Saying it out loud affirms this even more.

Another example? Well, I used to use the word "goals". I still do sometimes. But more often than not, I talk about what I am committed to. Why? Well, for me, goals indicates something that is far off, something that I haven't reached yet and something that I may or may not reach. Instead, when I say that I'm committed to writing a chapter of my book, it indicates to me personally what I can do today. Commitment is an active decision just made, an indication of who I am being at that very moment. So, my language reflects that. Of course, the follow through on my commitment indicates my seriousness, but that is the next step.

One more? Well, there was this great philosopher that I once read about. He went by the name of......Yoda! He said simply "Do or do not. There is no try!" Now, don't go skipping back through the pages to see if I used the word try. I really try not to. Oops. But do you get it? Performance. Do or do not. My language, my positive and clear language is part of the process. Now, GO and flip that language! Make it positive (+).

TODAY'S ACTION

1. Think about 3 words that you use regularly that are not affirming.

2. Write them down on an index card.

3. Place an X through them and then write a word that you will use in its place. (ex. Replace 'try' with 'do')

Day 24 - PRESS: The RIGHT Attitude

Pick Me-Up Line

Your attitude, not your aptitude, will determine your altitude.

- Zig Ziglar

Have you ever just gotten out of bed and you KNEW that your day was going to be bad because your attitude was horrible? Have you ever looked in the mirror and just said, "My attitude sucks rocks!!" No? Well, maybe that would be the honest truth of it. Many times, our day isn't bad because of the unexpected. It's bad because we chose not to prepare for how we were going to respond to life or because we chose not to CREATE the life that we wanted for that day. Now, when I talk about creating the life that you want, I'm not talking about money or a get rich scheme. I'm talking about waking up and the day being a beautiful day

simply because you SAID so.

The other day, I woke up and looked outside. What I saw was a pretty grey day. There were clouds in the sky. It had just rained and it looked like one of those days when most people would just rather be inside. But something came to my mind. I realized that I could still see. Nothing to do with blindness. I could still see. Now, as I science teacher, I realized that in order for me to see ANYTHING at all, there has to be light of SOME sort. If I'm outside in the daytime, that light source happens to be the sun. So, I reckoned that if I could see, then the sun was there somewhere. I couldn't really see it by looking out my window. But, even in the midst of the clouds, the sun still found a way to get enough light through for me to be able to see. I decided that I would focus on that, the fact that I could see and the fact that the sun was there. Because I made that decision, the day no longer began as a cloudy day. It began as a day that had a sun that was still overpowering the clouds even when they thought they won. That was MY story. That was MY focus. No one could make it any different because that was the attitude that I created. Yes, YOU create your attitude. You don't ever have to give that up.

But my kids, my spouse, my significant other, my friends, my parents, my family, they just get on my nerves.

Yes, probably very true. I mean, if you're putting your nerves out there in front of you, someone is BOUND to get on for a ride at some point. So, stop putting them out there. Choose your attitude. Create your story!

TODAY'S ACTION

1. On a piece of paper, write one thing that you
   want to create today. Make sure that it is
   something that you did not do yesterday.

2. Hold yourself accountable to this. Report to
   yourself at the end of the day. Did you fulfill
   your commitment?

Day 25 - PRESS: Embrace The Journey

Pick Me-Up Line

The purpose of life is to live it, to taste experience to the utmost, to reach out eagerly and without fear for newer and richer experience.

— Eleanor Roosevelt

I'd be lying if I said to you that I never get mad. I do. Not often, but it happens. I get annoyed sometimes as well. I have 3 kids so that's probably part of the package. I shouldn't but I'm human and so I mess up some times. The funny thing about being angry or annoyed is that I get angry or annoyed about things that have happened before. So, its not as if they are surprising to me. They have happened before. So, what on earth am I really getting angry or annoyed about? Here's an equation. Non-mounted flat screen TV + 2 year old + crayons + all in the same room = TV being written on. That's standard. My facts are pretty solid when it comes to researching this phenomenon. Yet, when it happens, I tend to get annoyed. Why? Another equation. My son dressed in his church clothes + walking to the car + puddles = A new outfit for church needed. Again, standard fare. I'm not sure why I would get annoyed or upset at this. Oh, I remember. I get upset because I have this story in my head that its not supposed to happen and my day is supposed to be perfect.

What I am learning is that life is not perfect. Things happen. They really do. And once they happen, there is absolutely no way for me to undo them. No rewind button. No "Back To The Future" time machine. Nope, nothing to save it. Nobody's coming! So, what do I need to do? Expect it and embrace it.

WHAT?? Expect bad things to happen? Expect to get annoyed? In other words, be a pessimist? Bro, didn't we just finish talking about positive language?

Why yes, yes we did. I'm saying that journeys are made up of hills and valleys. Everything has a time that it works and doesn't work. There is light and there is dark. Know that both will happen and embrace the journey. If you are in a storm, embrace it and know that there is good weather ahead at some point. If you are already in good weather, know that a storm will come at some point. Embrace that and then focus on the good weather after that. It's all just part of the journey.

TODAY'S ACTION

1. Write down something that made you upset recently.

2. What could you have done to avoid being upset? Write that down.

Day 26 - PRESS: Share & Inspire

Pick Me-Up Line

If your actions inspire others to dream more, learn more, do more and become more, you are a leader.

- John Quincy Adams

DON'T BE GREEDY!!! You just began to read and I'm already yelling at you! Sorry about that. Reminds me of my childhood. My mom used to give us a treat every so often. We learned how to make homemade onion dip using the onion soup mix and sour cream. Of course, each of us didn't have our own separate bowls. There was just one bowl in the middle of the table for myself and my two brothers. We would take the chips or carrots or whatever we were given and dive into the delicious dip.

The problems would begin when one of us was deemed by the other two to be scooping up too much of the dip on one chip. That's when the yelling would begin. DON'T BE GREEDY!! YOU'RE HOGGING THE DIP!! Of course, the yelling person would then proceed to demonstrate how much the 'appropriate' amount would be and very often there was disagreement about what was 'appropriate'. THAT'S STILL TOO MUCH!! Eventually, we started making our own little cups of dip. But, now that I think about it, the experience was never the same after that. There was something in the sharing part of it that brought a 'newness', an extra desire to the whole process of dip and chip eating. What is it about sharing?

Well, I haven't figured out the intricacies or chemical responses to sharing overall, but I do understand that with regard to your commitment, sharing can be a very beneficial thing. It does a few things:

- It lets people in to your world.

- It allows people to know what you are committed to and enthusiastic about.

- People will see what you are up to and look at their own lives for something comparative or better.

- It inspires them to action of their own (maybe not immediately, but they begin to think about it).

There is a level of accountability that comes with sharing. People that are inspired by your commitment seem to want to check in on how you are doing with it.

If they know what you are doing, they may be able to help or offer necessary resources.

If only for the accountability, share what you are doing with your friends, your family, your acquaintances. That tells people who you are committed to being, what you are excited and passionate about. This is helpful to YOU in your journey. But, it also serves other people as inspiration. So go ahead, get up, get on the phone, talk to somebody and tell them what you're about.

Tell them what you are committed to and change both of your lives!

TODAY'S ACTION

1. Be brave. Tell a total stranger today about your commitment.

Day 27 - Stay In Action

Pick Me-Up Line

Action is the foundational key to all success.

- Pablo Picasso

Have you ever heard the saying 'the race is not given to the swift or to the strong, but to the one who endures'? Every time I hear that saying, the story of The Turtle and The Rabbit comes to mind. (OK, so the story is actually called The Tortoise and the Hare, but I like mine a bit better.)

So, the story goes like this. There was this rabbit that absolutely LOVED to run. He was pretty fast and HE KNEW IT! So, every chance he got, he would tell every body how fast he was and then challenge them to a race. If people looked at him with any questioning, he would quickly jump up right in to their faces and yell, "HA!" He was yelling all over town until one day he saw a turtle walking by the bus stop. He noticed how slow the turtle was moving and began chuckling to himself, picturing scaring the turtle right out of his shell. He ran over to the turtle from behind, quickly jumped in front of him and yelled "HAAAAA!" Of course, the turtle didn't budge. He simply looked up at the rabbit with droopy eyes and slowly said, "Hey buddy." Again, the rabbit yelled, "HAAAAA". The turtle's only response was, "Why do you keep yelling like that?" The rabbit, getting a bit frustrated at his lack of impact, decided to try to embarrass the turtle. So, he said, "Dude, why are you walking so slowly anyway? I bet it takes you forever to get anywhere." The turtle simply quipped, "I get where I get when I get there but I get there." Confused and flustered, the rabbit decided that he wanted to embarrass the turtle and so he decided to challenge him to a race. He ran around putting up posters all over town. The posters featured him with a trophy and the turtle withdrawn into his shell.

Fast forward to race day. The gun sounds and the rabbit takes off. He runs for about 5 minutes and decides that he is so far ahead that the turtle can't ever catch up. He feels hungry so he hops over to a fast food joint and begins to order.

FOUR SLICES OF CARROT CAKE, WAITER! The waiter brings him his 4 slices and the rabbit dives in. He is on his third slice when he looks out the window and happens to see a bus driving by. In the front seat, he happens to see the turtle. So, he drops his cake and runs outside and runs after the bus. Run as he might, he is just too slow to keep up with a bus.

Moral? Don't stop to eat cake. Always keep it moving. Stay in action. Now, the traditional story talked about hard work, perseverance and pushing through methodically. That's true and that works. But, there are also other ways to get there. The point is, get there. Now, I realize that this story, my version at least, might lead you to think that I am endorsing cheating. Not at all. I simply wanted to tell a story about action in a different way. You were expecting, maybe, something more motivational? Nope. The simple point is keep it moving. It may not be in the way you expected or anyone else for that matter. But, stay in action. Don't stop. Most often, the journey is about picking up momentum. Stopping makes it harder to get back up to speed. Slowing down is still action. If you didn't get to do 30 minutes, do 10. If you didn't get to write 5 pages, write 1.5. Don't get disappointed. Don't beat yourself up or punish yourself. Just get back on track and KEEP IT MOVING. Stay in action!!

TODAY'S ACTION

1. Did you stay in action every day throughout this journey? If you missed a day, write down the cause of your miss.

2. Write down what you could've done differently that day.

Day 28 - Success Is A Lifestyle

Pick Me-Up Line

Develop success from failures. Discouragement and failure are two of the surest stepping stones to success.

- Dale Carnegie

There are two types of journeys. In the first journey, you reach your destination. However, there is a trip back to your original starting point. Then, there is the other type of journey when you are only going in one direction. You are not going back home or anywhere else because you are relocating and intending to stay in that new place. That type of trip is great because although you don't know what's ahead, you are excited about the possibilities and excited about this new place that you will call "home."

Success is the second journey. Change is the second journey. "Newness" is the second journey. What I love about this is that there is ALWAYS a destination on every journey. At each destination, you make a choice. Do you remain at that destination or do you build on it and plot a continued path? Do you become satisfied with that achievement or do you strive for something new? The great thing is that you can do whatever you choose. You create the destination. You create the journey. You create the story.

You have been creating a great story for 27 days and now

you have reached your destination. Yep, a new you. This is awesome by itself, but now you have opened up the door and you know that there is so much more. There is much more to you than you thought before. So, I'm not going to tell you what TO do, but I will mention what you CAN do. You CAN continue the lifestyle of success. You CAN continue the lifestyle of accomplishment. You CAN continue the lifestyle of "newness". You CAN continue to create a NEW YOU. This time, it only took you 28 days. Now, that wasn't so bad, was it?

TODAY'S ACTION

1. You remained committed for 28 days. What can you commit to next? Write down your new commitment.

Reading List

When I read my Bible, I pay attention to the verse in Ecclesiastes that says, "There is nothing new under the sun...." For me, that reminds me that although I may have put the pen to paper, many of the ideas were fed by something else or someone else. Some have been inspirations, some mentors, some were just things that I happened upon and enjoyed. But, they have contributed to me, to this book and to this process.

Here are some books from my reading list that have directly or indirectly contributed to this material.

Steve Chandler - 100 Ways To Motivate Yourself

Steve Chandler - Wealth Warrior

Charles Duhigg - The Power of Habit

Patrick Lencioni - Getting Naked

Lynne Twist - The Soul of Money

Napoleon Hill - Think & Grow Rich

David Allen - Getting Things Done

Tracey Goss - The Last Word on Power

Stephen Covey - The 7 Habits of Highly Effective People

Jim Collins - Good To Great

Dan S. Kennedy - No Rules: 21 Giant Lies About Success

Spencer Johnson - Who Moved My Cheese

Steven Pressfield - The War of Art

Rosamund Zander & Benjamin Zander - The Art of Possibility

About The Author

Robert Kennedy III is an educator, trainer, speaker, coach and author. His first book was published in 2012, Articulate Studio 09 Cookbook. This book was more technical in nature and related to specific software.

He started the 28 Days To A New Me process in 2012 and has helped people lose weight, write books, create new career paths, solidify their relationships both personal and spiritual. He consults with small businesses to help them craft success plans and understand technologies that help them to run an efficient businesses.

As a speaker, Robert speaks on the topics of perseverance, personal development and success, and technology for small business startup.

He has been married to his wife, Nadia, for 12 years and has 3 awesome kids. He currently resides in Baltimore County, Maryland. He makes time to play basketball, softball, golf, as well as keyboard and guitar.

To find out more about Robert, you can visit his blog at: http://www.robertkennedy3.com.

For speaking engagements, you may contact him at inquiries@robertkennedy3.com.

You may also connect with him online at:

Facebook: http://www.facebook.com/robertkennedyiii

Twitter: @robertkennedy3

Made in the USA
San Bernardino, CA
16 October 2018